In *Elemental*, Scott Owens has crafted poems of praise and witness that connect me more deeply to the world and to my own heart. The language is both elegant and precise, that is to say, elemental. "I'm here for the trees," begins one poem, and then in another, he writes about eating wild strawberries, "little else could make me feel more alive." These poems explore the natural world with wonder, curiosity, and astonishment. Like any good naturalist, Owens looks and sees deeply, asks questions, makes connections, and shares with the reader what he learns. Whether it is through the lens of a mature gardener elbow-deep in earth or a traveler venturing into new terrain, these poems bring the reader to a place where "everyone remembers/what it means to live."

-Pat Riviere-Seel, author of *Because I Did Not Drown*

It's all happening here. Just look: *after rain the hills / fill up with mist, everything / else just memory*. Just?! Perhaps the mist is forgetfulness, perhaps ignorance or willful turning away, nevertheless mist must part and memory stride out into the open, called forth by the elemental poetry of Scott Owens. *Elemental* is seeking, discovery, self-revelation, assurance; Scott shares with us his essentials, those things in life possible to trust and to love. Shape of tree, breath of breeze, turning season, end of days – from these lines may we each stride out to discover our own home on this earth.

-Bill Griffin, naturalist and poet at **Verse & Image** (griffinpoetry. com)

Scott Owens delves deep into the simple but precious things we take for granted and opens our eyes, to see what he sees, what he hears, and feels, to bring into consciousness those elemental parts of life. An emotionally intelligent person, he lives and breathes poetry, and we are the fortunate recipients. In this book, Scott's diversity of poetry rings out. Places from Arizona to Hayesville, NC, from the death of his beloved dog to Haiku. Each page takes us on a journey. We are eager to see where we will go next.

-Glenda Beall, author of *Now Might As Well Be Then*

Elemental

Poems

Scott Owens

REDHAWK
PUBLICATIONS

ELEMENTAL
Copyright © 2025 Scott Owens

ISBN: 979-8-89933-002-5 (Paperback)
Library of Congress Control Number: 2025942823

Cover Design (Art): Erin Mann
Cover Photo: Richard McGee
Book Design: Erin Mann

Printed in the United States of America.
First printing 2025.

Redhawk Publications
The Catawba Valley Community College Press
2550 Hwy 70 SE
Hickory NC 28602
https://redhawkpublications.com

I don't know exactly what a prayer is.
I do know how to pay attention.

Mary Oliver

. . . let the soft animal of your body
love what it loves.

Mary Oliver

Also by Scott Owens

- *Holding Holden* (Redhawk, 2025)
- *eventually*: haiku, Illustrated by Missy Cleveland (Redhawk, 2024)
- *An Augury of Birds*, Collaboration with Photographer, Clayton Joe Young (Redhawk, 2024)
- *Round Here: Images From and Near Catawba County*, Collaboration with Photographer, Clayton Joe Young (Redhawk, 2023)
- *All In: A Novel of Love in Poetry*, Collaboration with Poet, Pris Campbell (Redhawk, 2023)
- *Prepositional: Selected and New Poems* (Redhawk, 2022)
- *Worlds Enough: Poems for Children (and a few grown ups)*, Collaboration with Artist, Missy Cleveland (Redhawk, 2022)
- *Sky Full of Stars and Dreaming* (Redhawk, 2021)
- *Counting the Ways* (Main Street Rag, 2020)
- *Down to Sleep* (Main Street Rag, 2016)
- *Thinking About the Next Big Bang in the Galaxy at the Edge of Town* (Main Street Rag, 2015)
- *To* (Main Street Rag, 2014)
- *Eye of the Beholder* (Main Street Rag, 2013)
- *Shadows Trail Them Home*, Collaboration with Poet, Pris Campbell (Clemson University Press, 2012)
- *For One Who Knows How to Own Land* (Future Cycle Press, 2012)
- *Country Roads: Travels Through Rural North Carolina*, Collaboration with Photogapher Clayton Joe Young (2012)
- *Something Knows the Moment* (Main Street Rag, 2011)
- *The Nature of Attraction*, collaboration with Pris Campbell (Main Street Rag, 2010)
- *Paternity* (Main Street Rag, 2010)
- *The Fractured World* (Main Street Rag, 2008)
- *Book of Days* (Dead Mule, 2009)
- *Deceptively Like a Sound* (Dead Mule, 2008)
- *The Persistence of Faith* (Sandstone, 1994)

ACKNOWLEDGMENTS

Grateful acknowledgment is given to the following journals where some of these poems were first published.

Blue Fifth Review for "March with Your Flowers Burning."
Caesura for "Castings."
Charlotte Poetry Review for "Outer Beaches."
Crucible for "February's Air of Waiting."
Dead Mule School of Southern Poetry for "Book of Days."
Georgia Journal for "November Never Speaks of Itself."
Iodine for "Elemental."
Kansas Quarterly for "Because Trees Had Always Meant Escape."
*Ken * Again* for "Camping."
Main Street Rag for "Discoveries Made Late in Life."
Mind in Motion for "December's Ground Freezes, Shrinks, Cracks, Thaws, Swells with Forgotten Water, Pushes to the Surface Rocks, Seeds, Things Buried, Reborn."
North American Review for "July, the Sun, and Thundering Storms."
Notes from the Gean for [hours after weeding], and [last day at the beach]
Pembroke for "Listening to Louie in the Shadow of Grandfather."
Phase & Cycle for "At 6000 Feet."
Pirene's Fountain for [afternoons you fear], [fields of vision], "Waiting for Wings at Wiseman's View."
Radiant Turnstile for "Cycles," and "Missing Autumn, Missing Leaves, Missing All that Falling Finds You Open as Trees."
Right Hand Pointing for "Stopping in Woods."
Sketchbook for [August day].
Stone Pile for "Finding Home."

Town Creek Poetry for "Clearing the Garden."
Verse Image for "All That Is," and "Of Mint and Memory."
Wild Goose Poetry Review for "Gradually the Summer Leaves."
Willows Wept Review for [after rain the hills], "Barrier Islands,"
    "A Moment in the Life," "A Plague of Ladybugs."
Word Salad for [traffic stopped]
Your Daily Poem for "August without Fanfare," and "Pansies."

CONTENTS

Travelogue

Discoveries Made Late in Life

Any New Thing That Matters

Finding Home

When you moved around as much as we did,
it's hard to know where to call home.
I always go back to two green houses
on a red hill near a place called Stony Point,

the fields full of rocks and cows, a place
I lived maybe two summers of my childhood,
coming back a week or a month
at a time when money or men ran out.

What made it home was how it never
changed, same people, same
ruined houses, falling barn,
tireless cars in boundless pastures,

seven acres with no rules
but what we made, no expectations,
no one watching, fields and woods,
and the room to be anyone I wanted to be.

Elemental

Having been raised in shadow of pecan trees
he learned to keep his insecurities
concealed in shells the color of earth, almost
inextricable and gathered in brown paper bags.

Having been shaped by twisted logic of weather
in South Carolina's Tornado Alley,
he learned when to move with wind and when
to stand fast and howl against the blow.

Having been dipped in yellow water
without being held by anything but current
he learned to sink to the bottom, plant his feet
in mud below and walk back to shore.

Having been burned in fires of passion and forgiveness,
faith and disbelief, he learned to trust little
but what he could see: bird flight, dirt
beneath the nails, quiet eternity of mountain.

BOOK OF DAYS

January Looks Forward and Back, Feeds the Stove
October's Wood, Saves the Ashes for April's Garden

January wraps trees in sleeves
of ice, coats the ground in frost,
throws its shawl of morning mist
on field and lake and stream.

January plants sage and lavender,
costmary and mint, pulls up fingers
of crocus and daffodil, green
buds of forsythia, rose, spirea.

January's voice is cold and coarse—
the silver moon, the blue sky,
the gray sky, the absinthe moon,
the empty trees, the trees filled

with cedar waxwings. January
wears out darkness sleeping late,
puts on morning's half-white face,
speaks of what is bare and necessary.

It is dangerous to know the mind
of January. January is life
and death, the new born from the chest
of the old, half-formed eyes of flowers

forcing their way through tight skin
of limbs, mouths of bulbs tonguing
up through dirt, opening to earth
and sky and air of January.

February's Air of Waiting

February, his feet by a fire,
warms the morning's chill away,
huddles under horsehair, bearskin,
eats savory, spinach, and sweet
marjoram, cradles a book of days
in his hands, wearily scratches

in plans of days to come. Scratching
in ashes, February stokes the fire,
watches flames the color of day
speak, roar, sing their way
to dying, listens to the thick, sweet
sound of wood burning, to skins

of black ash, dry, skinny
sticks, half-dead limbs scratching
against each other, green wood sweating,
snapping, spitting into the fire,
life consumed with eating away
its own body and lighting the days

of February's interiors. Such days,
kept wrapped in thick skins
of house and cloak, await the sweet
sounds of newborn spring scratching
at windows, sun's warmth firing
panes to melting, sweeping away

the ground's cover of ice, sweetening
the air with labor's harsh perfume. Today
February can only bank the fire,
gather limbs, hang skins
to dry, absently scratch

blades on whetstones, put the tools away.

Outside the world goes winter's way,
hedges white with malignant sweetness,
limbs full of irritable scratching,
wind howling at the day,
earth drinking its icy skin,
trees lit with frostian fire.

Sprout-kale, month-long day of waiting,
sweet season of keeping beneath the skin,
I will scratch my way through your consumptive fire.

March with Your Flowers Burning

Just as I had gotten things under
control again, you showed up,
with your head in the clouds,
your eyelids full of rain,
your cuffs of late snow,
your feet tracking mud,

you who refuse to be ruled,
you with your willow's strand
of pearls, you with your fingers
sucking scilla, daffodil, crocus,
your nostrils stuffed with snot,
your cheeks puffed,
your lips dripping lullabies,
your rainbow-wicked smile,

you with your forsythia switch,
your many-voweled throat, your mind
like black ice, your hands always
open, the slap and plea, the cup
and howl, the easy lure,
the careless jangle of trees.

How could I hope to respond,
my arms grown thin, eyes
winter-blind, hands
unaccustomed to such change?

You were the one I dreamed of,
with your mouth full of promises,
your cheeks honey-smeared,
your hands around my balls.

Rush of April Coming In

Schizophrenic April rained the ceiling down
pulled up lamb's ear and fennel columbine and sage
ran the radio outdoors the clouds transforming
the hills running mud my feet slippery wet
on steps sweating thick socks tracking criss-
crossed patterns of yellow earth the architecture
of days sprouting green lines across the sky
running streams between brick beside the road
across the yard in pools of sunshine dripping
puddles beneath the trees cold fingers raking
sky white gray blue or black and flowers blooming
anyway April's cruelest joke not enough to stop
their show of colors only slightly mud-spattered
the way they clean themselves like cats in windows
waiting for mid-month to burst open as mouths
to weather warming with winter's burning away.

Of Flowered Gardens as in May

You've been working the garden again
to the texture you want, beating it
with mattock and hoe, pulling up what
you won't grow, putting down what you will.

Everything you do leaves a different taste
in your mouth. Pulling up ivy is nothing
like pulling up myrtle. Rooting one only
like the other in the earth you turn.

These are days with high foreheads
and Roman noses coming out of the ground,
with eyebrows bushy as clouds, with green hands
of limbs stroking the windows open,

with the too-cool sauntering in of May.
You sniff the air alive with spring's ammonia,
search for the living bloom of earth
beneath stones. In the garden bitter drops

of May hang beneath umbrella leaves,
the screaming plant, the little man.
Loosestrife, spiderwort, bleeding hearts
blaze their public weeping. Squirrels swing

from cats' mouths. Birds lie dead on the path,
premature bodies pink as velvet gloves.
Lichen slices through rock. You arrive
with your hands full of little graves,

your thoughts full of the deaths of planting.
Immature May, May with its half-hearted
promises, May the almost ripe, has called

you to its secret rooms full of flowers,

to its life dripping from fingertips
of leaves. You will open the earth again.
You will set the seedling in place
and feed it with your own cracked hands.

June Arrives, Dressed in Grace and Pain

Hesitant, June stood waiting on the horizon for days,
then walked in with an uncertain limp,
dragging the dead heads of spring behind it.

Now it stands staring into fields that will not grow,
counts fallen fingers of foxglove, sits in the trees
at night wilting the leaves, spreading its heat around.

Now it sings in the throats of mockingbirds at night,
in distant whippoorwills teasing you out into darkness
towards dead-leaf bodies you'll never find.

There is no loneliness like June's confusion
of faces, bee-balm's foolscap of red, yarrow's
cowardly hands, bright, boasting tongues of gladiolus.

In the day edible orange daylilies open their mouths
to a sky full of promises. At night the air shines
with bodies burning to touch one another.

The angel of June flies into the room, black wings,
red belly spiraling down to black, three-part-body
you can't help but want on top of you.

July, the Sun, and Thundering Storms

July in the sun, a straw hat tilted
on his head, gathers catalpa worms for fishing,
plucks many-lobed moons of blackberries
from a green sky, briars pulling blood
from fingers and wrists, mixing purple-sweet
juices in the red palette of his palm.

Cold shower flagellations, mornings
as warm as noon, green oppression of leaves,
hands that hold you tighter than regret,
days that take you back to feet dangling
from fence posts, tailgates, low bridges,
sunlight, the taste of plums at 2 A.M.

July spends days spread out by a stream,
lounged beneath a tree, picking clover,
watching thunder and no rain rumble
into darkness, watching night rise
from the ground, buzz lethargic with life,
glow in slow erratic circles.

July's black jacket of sleep descends,
legs coated yellow with dreams,
with pre-transformation of flowers.
Hibiscus buds pucker like mouths,
tremble with giving, quiver beneath
forgotten hands plying them open.

Hummingbird tongues this petaled throat,
laps up yellow dust of the past,
eases out hum of skies talking
at night, loves this face to shape
of cups, hands to wings, dreams
to distant islands of your eye.

August Without Fanfare

August blew his flute in the shade,
lay down by the water, kicked off his shoes,
put his feet up, refused to care
about money, time, the national debt.

August lounged on tree limbs,
hung tires from branches, fell in love
with water, played break the wave,
jump the wave, ride the wave in.

August faced the horizon with indifference,
waited for pecans to fall, muscadines
to turn, trumpet vines to sound
their wild annunciations.

August proclaimed the fish in the trees,
the cleavage of shadows, the stars
shooting holes in the sky,
God in his glass-bottomed boat.

For once the dog days of August
were not dog days at all
but children running through woods,
warming their mouths with words

unafraid to be spoken. August
sang to mockingbirds' random chants,
pressed his face into crepe myrtles,
wore mimosa in his hair, scratched his name

into trunks of trees. August made friends
with everyone, fed the birds,
watered the plants, wanted to give

his bread to the child in the street.

August came in without fanfare,
stayed its requisite number of days,
colored the night bright with stars,
left us the resurrection of children.

September Sits in Too Big Shoes

crown askew, parasol twirling,
face powdered white as dawn,
nails pushed back to moon-shaped cuticles,
painted red as chrysanthemums.

September opens her hands to everything,
tries on summer's bright blouse,
autumn's dappled skirt,
winter's cloak of darkness.

In cool September we began again
the lives we thought we'd live,
cut the nets beneath us, healed
the oldest scars. I said forever

and saw for once the way time
didn't matter. You said yes,
this is the way and led me there.
I felt the blows, for the first time,

like they belonged to me, took them
inside, cried to think of all
I'd forgotten. There is no happiness
like September's salvation: sweep and swell

of blackbirds, coagulation of shadows.
September's eyes fill with things turning,
weather and peaches, walnuts and plums,
leaves stitched with remnants of color.

With little sense of why, September
saves everything, gathers rain
in bottles, picks up sticks,
presses leaves into shapes of hands.

October's Reign of Yellow Leaves

Outside, leaves fall like blackbirds descending,
summer's bright oppression seeming just
begun already ending.

The trees are having their annual falling out.
October tracks mud in the house, kneels
on grass-stained knees.

Dead stalks of flowers, smell of leaves
burning, dream fragments like chips of moon
slipping off the horizon.

October's drizzle of days pushes the sky
together again, its distant expanse appearing
through blank terror of trees.

Night's white mask of cold, morning's
lingering wet breath, black earth
whispering exhumed corpses.

As the last leaves fall, October goes out,
rattling chains, knotting trees with blackbirds,
swelling with echoes of leaving.

November Never Speaks of Itself

gathers wood, kills the boar,
lets December say what cold
the winter holds, whispers only
silver flashes in the spring,
cleaning away what green still
clings to rock or limb.

November sits smirking, indifferent,
watching each displeasure
like something not a part of its own,
watching everything washing
out to gray, every bit of color
giving way to December's coming on.

November never speaks of itself,
makes use of all that autumn brings it,
tamps down leaves beneath quiet
rains, hushes what sings, sends birds'
black streaming across the sky,
lets every night grow longer.

December's Ground Freezes, Shrinks, Cracks, Thaws, Swells with Forgotten Water, Pushes to the Surface Rocks, Seeds, Things Buried, Reborn

Each day I look to see what has risen,
arrowhead, skull of a bird, crocus bulb.
It may be nothing. It may be everything
I've wanted. One day I found seven rocks
almost all the same, like shattered pieces
of the same stone. Other times I find glass,
keys, fragments of things whose meaning only
the earth remembers. It's no wonder Christ rose,
the way the ground pushes things out like water.

The earth has hardened its water to stone.

Turning rough crystals of dirt I feel
as far now from changing as I have ever been.
I wonder if the ground will open its arms
to take me in, if the earth will want this body
I've ruined, if it still can clean these bones
of all the things I've thrown onto them.

I wonder if there is time enough
to change before the changing begins.

SOUTHERN SEASONS

A Moment in the Life

Lying beside the stream, bare feet barely touching
the water, touching everywhere the water has been.
Hands turn clover to left and right in streams of grass,
bright stars of dandelions. I think of the past,
of things that lie buried in the earth in the green birth
of spring. There are mostly people here.
If I'd started with people, their faces would have turned
to flowers, and flowers to earth and water and sky.
I think of the future I am drawn into. There are mostly
people here, their faces blooming with wonder.
Lying beside the stream, bare feet barely touching
the water, touching everywhere the water has yet to go.

The Appreciation of Mockingbirds

Life would be so much sweeter
if we could all be like mockingbirds

(happy with what god has given us,
flashing wings in appreciation,
fanning tails, leaping up,
flaunting bright patches,
singing songs of celebration
at the top of our lungs
in a diversity of voices
without concern for who hears
or what they think)

23 hours a day.

It's only at 6:00 a.m.
that mockingbirds are not appreciated.

A Plague of Ladybugs

Certainly not Biblical in its proportions,
no sharply angled legs, no alien
faces extruding grasshopper spit,
only a fraction the size,

almost cute, but for the feeling
of six legs on the back of your neck,
in your hair at night, the sense
of constant motion at the edge of sight,

and I am no Charlton Heston
promising milk and honey,
but eighty ladybugs
sucked up in one day

in the vacuum's crevice attachment
and forty or more every day for weeks
is enough to give anyone the creeps,
make them long for an exodus of their own.

Gradually the Summer Leaves

Gradually the summer leaves
yellow, harden beneath autumn's
drying wind, drift to piles for burning.
Each leaf you see reminds you
of something you hadn't planned,
something that moves on without you.

Another week and sound will travel
like leaves over housetops, through
trees grown bare with falling.

Each day the earth grows duller,
the sky grows larger, putting
itself together like a jigsaw,
one piece at a time.

Each night the wind smells
like somewhere you haven't been
and are not ready to go.

                                  Plum
              met
                                                      ting
  to
                        the
                                                dry
          earth

                    s   s
                   h   r
                  a   e
                   tt

                with a splat
              absorbed by dirt

Missing Autumn, Missing Leaves, Missing All that Falling Finds You Open as Trees

Autumn happened while our backs
were turned, so we missed the sky
blackening with birds, we missed
the leaves turning to burning
sheets of color, we missed the ground
covering itself with fallen things.

Autumn hung in the trees for weeks,
then fell when we weren't looking,
so we missed the dust of flowers
on our faces, we missed the air
turning cool on our skin, the sky drawn
towards night's single point of closing.

We know it didn't happen
overnight, and yet it seems so.
Caught up in our lives we look
up this morning and see the sun
shining through limbs grown thin
with leaving, sharp with falling.

Not even autumn's rough rustling
could wake us from our sleep, not even
this weeping of trees could move us
to hear, not even the wind's choired
voices could make us see the sky
put on its mask of darker days.

Only now, when autumn has grown
places without leaves, skies
without ending, do we look up
and see the limbs of any tree

above any house and think
of those we've known since childhood:

here the pine we climbed, our legs
smeared yellow with sap; here
the oak's broad umbrella frame;
here mimosa's silk now nothing but sticks;
here the pecan we threw ropes over
and shook until we ran from the falling.

Cycles

Rain falls slowly
a thousand times,
pushes light to the ground,
kicks mud in its face,
raises rust from inside
abandoned cars.
Metal flakes, like leaves,
spin imperceptibly
to the ground running
away unnoticed in rain
falling slowly
a thousand times.

Turn your back.
Trees shed,
bud again.
Buildings collapse.
Earth erodes.
Roads travel
their separate journeys,
never arriving
at the same place twice.
Faces prune,
appear again,
same nose,
mouth, eyes.
Flowers open
and close, open
and close, turn
to the ground.

Rain falls slowly
a thousand times.

Clouds open
and close, open
and close. What rises
washes away. The sun's
circle of day breaks,
drips into darkness,
runs toward dawn's
spreading out again.

Howling at Sirens

The neighbor's dog, who never gets walked,
never goes in, lives all day, every day,
in a small, fenced-in backyard,
only seeing anyone or anything else
twice a day when they feed him,
howls at sirens, his one trick,
or the one allowed him, and a charming one at that.
I watch him sometimes through gaps and knotholes
in the hardwood fence, a beautiful husky,
pale-eyed, thick-furred. I speak to him sometimes.
He barks, whines, moves to the other side
of the yard, paces back and forth,
stopping occasionally to stare at the slats
of the fence like Rilke's panther at the bars.
I feel I should do something, but I don't know what.
I've tried to visit, but he's not a friendly dog,
and my neighbor's not a friendly person.
I've called the police, but they say if he has shelter
and is being fed, then it's not abuse.
I wonder how much like him we might be,
trapped by the limitations of our own
perception, unable to see what lives
beyond. After a moment's distraction
and still no idea what to do,
I go back inside, sit in the familiar chair,
turn on the news, and yell at the screen.

Stopping in Woods

Sometimes the noise of the world
rankles me so much that I get in my car
and drive as far away from the city
as time allows until I find
a dirt road half grown over, clearly
not much in use, probably made
by hunters or the power company or loggers,
and I turn down that road and go until
I find a tree I can pull under,
and I roll down the windows, turn off
the car, lie back, close my eyes
and half sleep, half dream,
half listen to almost nothing
and the possibility of rest.

Wood Thrush

Much more often heard than seen,
hermited here between the trees,
brown body blending in among fallen leaves,
even its name sounds serene.
Streaks on breast like sheet music
or dappled light through twisted limbs,
lyric rise and fall of haunting song
as much a part of Southern woods
as yellow poplar, rhododendron,
all that calls to men like me,
watchers lured out in hopes to see
this source of endless mystery.

Night in the Forest

You hear every twig snap,
every leaf flutter, every
strange unknowable animal sound.
Looking, your eyes widen,
Find bits of light to hold onto,
see shadows move from shadows
in the slightest breath of wind.

You smell animal musk,
taste it in the air,
feel the hair on your arms,
the back of your neck, rise
as you're certain something
comes closer. Every sense
is filled to overflowing.

And yet amidst the unease,
the urge to panic,
there is also in moments of stillness
a calm, a sense of peace
of no obligation, no schedule to attend,
you only ever feel here
in the still, in the quiet, in the dark.

Birds Are Real

When I was six I told my mother
that birds were like flowers in the air.
Since then I've observed the habits
of more than 400 species of birds.
I've seen the sublime dive of osprey,
heard the pointless laughter of kookaburra,
watched the murmurations of starlings
across a twilight sky, trembled
before a siege of 30 herons
camped outside a fish house in Destin, Florida.
And this summer off the coast of Nova Scotia
I saw huge flocks of puffins for the first time,
birds that spend their life at sea,
only coming among us to breed.

Conspiracy theorists and those who mock
conspiracy theorists can argue
whether birds are real or not,
but any poet will tell you,
any artist, musician, naturalist,
student of aeronautics, anyone
who has ever tended a wounded bird,
peered into a nest, touched the broken open
speckled blue shell, admired
song, or wing, or flight, can tell you
that birds are palpably, audibly,
joyfully, decidedly real,
more real than love or hope, fear or distrust,
any airy abstractions we devise to explain ourselves.

Huck's Last Walk

You extend your front legs
and spread them wide to get
your nose down to
and into the concrete to smell,
your one remaining sense,
everything that has come before you.
You struggle to pull yourself back up,
stumble forward, fall
to the left. I help you up.
You press against my leg
to keep your balance and bearing,
stumble forward again,
discover the nandina to the side
of the walkway, and press your nose,
and then your entire head
into the bush to inhale
everything that has been here already,
as if this map of smells
could bring life back to you.
15 years of companionship,
of joy, and experience, and breathing in
everything that life has to offer,
only the last a series
of constantly new challenges,
deafness, lameness, confusion,
loss of cognitive function.
Still, despite the difficulties
it brings me nothing but joy
to share with you now this last walk,
this last act of love.

I Had to Kill My Old Dog Huck

I had to kill my old dog Huck today.
I say my dog, but he was everyone's dog really,
at least everyone who ever met him.
He was a good dog, *the best dog ever*,
everyone would say, and I had to agree.
He used to lie under the table at the Farmers' Market
with just his head and front feet sticking out
from beneath the tablecloth so passers by
might reach down and pet him, and he would
sort of lean into the pet so the person petting
would know just how much it meant to him.
And he'd let children take his toys or food,
pull his hair, sit on him without complaint
or merest suggestion of reaction. And he had
such an easy way about him, such gentle eyes,
that he could turn the most vicious dog
into a docile pup. *One in a million*, they say.
When we'd take him hiking he'd run ahead
just far enough that we could still see him
and then run back to make sure we were okay.
Only once when he flushed a nest of grouse
on accident did he not come from wherever he was
at the slightest whistle or whisper of his name.
Fifteen years a companion, he had just gotten
too old, couldn't hear, couldn't run,
struggled to stand up, couldn't hardly understand
what it was you wanted from him,
but still tried to make you happy
by doing whatever he thought he could figure out.
Somehow it seemed he would always be in the world,
and now the world is not the same.
I had to kill my old dog Huck today.
He was a good dog, the best dog ever.

Some Things We Do with Little Chance of Success

I drive through the cemetery,
shortcut to avoid afternoon
carpool at the elementary school,
but more hoping to see
the foxes I saw the first time
on a winter day 5 years ago
with my daughter, heads on a swivel,
ears piqued and listening,
gorgeous tails trailing behind.
I've seen them three times since then.
About one out of every 100 times
I've cut through. One percent,
unlikely probability but one
worth taking the chance to see.

Restoration

Christmas morning.
Sorry, she says,
you had to clean up
alone.
I tell her,
It has been a good morning:
two foxes, a kinglet,
the white-throated sparrows,
everything back in place.

16 Haiku

ground covered in snow
purple crocuses stretch necks
towards winter's white sun

February dawns
patchy and ragged –
all there is half thawed

after rain the hills
fill up with mist, everything
else just memory

the moon shines by no
light of its own, still burning
through obscurity

traffic stopped along
the highway shoulder
mimosa trees bloom

last day at the beach
content with watching
almost no waves

certain summer days
stretch dry and mean, heat clinging
to everything

afternoons you fear
such heat will never end—
all at once the rain

August day blows in
through open windows—
shower of birch seeds

drenched in dreams
of autumn, who would wake
so willingly

Appalachian chill
early September — colors
beginning to turn

fields of vision
begin to open
confetti of leaves

traffic sounds outside
my window — wind blows fallen
leaves across the road

cold arrives
on quiet feet—
November's held breath

tips of balsam fir
brushed with white – the year's
first sign of aging.

full moon –
brightest ornament
in a Christmas sky

a priori

Murmuration, sussuration, evanescence,
the sound of words like a hundred birds
flowing through the sky like water,
like a shoal of fish in the water,
seemingly unguided, twisting
and turning almost as one, as if
directed by a single discernible
mind, the one undetectable, perhaps
not existing at all but just
a communal intuition older
than individual birds, older
than generations even, from a time
before the waters above
the firmament, the waters below
the firmament were ever divided at all.

Ammon's Stump

He'd be the first to tell you
he didn't cut that tree down.
Storm took it,
broke it off 8 ft above the ground
where it stood knee deep in Brasstown Creek.
Others would tell you too
when they weren't jealous of the haul
he constantly brought up out of there.
He'd admit to taking the chainsaw and trimming it
down to the perfect sitting height for fishing
and that's where you could find him
from early morning almost any day
catching supper without standing in water
or slipping on muddy slopes.

Southern Seasons

Late March, tenderest green
of spring contrasts with purple redbuds,
white pears, fall's foreshadow
of red maples, yellow poplars
just beginning to bud out.

Can anything be as bright as June?
Days lengthening, light lasting
longer, as if the month exists
mainly to show us just how loud
the mouths of flowers might be.

October evening expresses itself
through irrepressible flow of leaves
falling down and around, filling sky
and ground with every color ever
imagined or ever needed to.

Sometimes it's unclear which
is the art and which the canvas,
late December's symmetry
of bare limbs, or the clear blue
putting itself together beyond.

I could have started this with any day.
There's hardly any time of year
we're not provided enough beauty
to keep us going, keep us inspired,
keep us believing in the goodness of it all.

TRAVELOGUE

Waiting for Wings at Wiseman's View
(Linville, NC)

Seeing this
how could he not feel
he was meant to fly,
the clouds beneath him,
the mountains laid out
before him like stepping stones.

Surely, he thinks, his arms,
as well, could cup the air
beneath them, translate
thermals to lift, glide
across almost visible currents,
like floating on water,
spreading your weight
across a thin surface of ice.

The only sound is the fluttering
percussion of wings
fingering the sky, searching
for edges, the out and back
of his own breath stretched
taut between two fields
of air rising beneath him.

Here there is only the waiting
that has been here ten million years
or longer. He opens his arms
to it. He opens his hands,
mouth, eyes. He takes in
all that he can as one thing
and stands upright, leaning
as far as mortality allows,
whispering the silent prayer of waiting.

Outer Beaches
(Waves, NC)

Two lights shine in silent, slow chase across
the horizon before the sun's first pink spreads out.
Last night the tide rose its highest in years.
This morning it falls back the same extreme.

Night of the big moon they call it — rare coordination
of perigee and opposition — moon tracing the sun's
exact track across the sky, sitting full of water
on wave tops, then shrinking through its arc of ascent.

This morning we walk the beach to see what the moon
has pulled from its own mirror image, what such
mitotic birth brings forth: string of whelk egg cases,
rusted tachometer, driftwood the shape of the state
of Georgia, angel wings neither of us can wear.

This morning we watch the sun roll out like an eye
held open too long, watch gulls keep a frightened space
between us, open their wings to strafing of wind,
kite across sand to another nervous perch.

Shipwrecked islands rise in the distance, sea grass,
marsh hawk, ruddy turnstones. We walk far enough apart
to scan the width of beach, feel wind shiver between us.
Waves saunter in as if nothing could stop them,
their slow motion repeated in your lashes' rise and fall.

Haiku
(Joshua Branch, NC)

mountain spring—
though the river runs away
it never leaves

Stack Rock Creek
(Linville, NC)

One has to wonder
how they got there,
what hands placed them
one atop another
just so to create
a wall in water
or several walls
that also create
ledge after ledge
and pools gathering
behind them until
the water spills
over, cascading
into the next
pool below,
whether it could
possibly be
a single pair
of hands, a single
day or year,
and whether
they had to be
worked and reworked
as the water changed,
the hands changed,
the things carried
by the water, sometimes
displacing them, sometimes
making them disappear
altogether, changed,
whether it served
a purpose, making

things stand
still
if only a moment
to be seen better,
gathering, collecting,
saving for reflection,
or use, or merely
the possibility
of appreciation.

The Demand for Form
(Pea Island, NC)

These footprints I leave behind
form a faulty pattern. Uneven steps
leave uneven gaps of sand
or crooked lines where I've dodged
the tide. My instep arch refuses
to sink as low as heel or toes,
and my second toe extends beyond
its rightful place in the rightful slope of toes.
No matter, the sea quickly erases
any proof of my passing, preferring
the smoother lines it leaves behind,
reducing every track I might have made
to what it was before, unaccountable
abundance, uniformity of absence.

At 6000 Feet
(Mt. Mitchell, NC)

Reaching the top
there is nowhere
to go, but down.
The trees know this
but resist.
Bare branches
strain against
the great pane
of sky, searching
for a single crack
to slip through.

Weathered trunks
are barely enough
to hold what lies
above them,
their flattened heads
seem always about
to break beneath
heaven's oppression,
but don't
remaining always
barely enough.

haiku
(Balsam, NC)

silent night driving
alone – shadow of the earth
pulled across the moon

haiku
(Pamlico Sound, NC)

before the kayak
sky and sound have become one
thing — the storm breaks

haiku
(Emerald Isle, NC)

moonlight on water—
a winding path no evil
spirit could follow

haiku
(Ocracoke Island, NC)

sunlit morning clouds,
great blue heron overhead—
never too far gone

Barrier Islands
(Hatteras Village, NC)

Three stories up on a rail at the south end
of Hatteras, I watch ferries come and go
taking their cargo of vacationers, one-day
diners, to more remote Ocracoke,
twenty miles of beach, sand, mosquitoes,
building up to hotel-studded Silver Lake,
artificial harbor said to be Edward Teach's
final hideaway before hanging, seabirds
and high tiders the only permanent residents.

On the other side, the ocean seems
to flow north, Gulfstream current
bringing enough warm water in which to swim,
double sandbar making it clearer
than I've ever seen this far north.
Sport fishermen cruise up and down
this coastline all day, hauling in
cobia, mackerel, drum. At night
I see their lights, singular in a sea
of darkness, sometimes hear voices
pitched just right to pierce
the constant roll of surf.

None of us leave much of a mark
on islands known to be temporary
themselves, migrating west,
shaped and reshaped by blue-green
waters of the Atlantic, patrolled
by timeless squads of gull
and tern, grackle and skimmer.
Footprints are washed or blown away

by nightfall, words drowned in wind
and waves, everything else
consumed by time as counted
in the constancy of sea.

Camping
(Natural Bridge, KY)

After the rain
everything is clean
and new again,
trees heavy with life,
sky opening
and a rainbow
proclaiming good
intentions,
the quiet filled
with awe.

Rainbow Falls
(Mt. Le Conte, TN)

The rain began as we started back down
the mountain, soft at first, then steady,
then everywhere at once. The ground
that had seemed stone moments before
turned into mud, stream, torrent
coursing its way back toward where
we'd climbed the arduous hours of morning.

We sought shelter beneath thick
clumps of rhododendron, rock
ledges, but nothing kept out the rain.
Even our clothes designed to resist
water became saturated and useless,
mere rags to be removed and wrung out.

We just kept going.
There was nothing else to do,
shoes soaked through, slogging
through water above our ankles,
half blinded by rain,
dodging trees that became visible
only with our hands reached out to find them.

It felt at first, frightening,
then miserable, and finally, oddly, a release
to know that nothing we did mattered,
to know the best and worst of what
we were, what we tried, what
we were capable of, were all one
to the rain, to the trees,
to the thousand thousand years of mountain.

Painted Desert
(Arizona)

Ten million years a river
ran here,
bearing silt, trees, life.
200 million more,
nothing,
wood turning to stone,
stone to powder,
powder to dust,
lifeless beauty
refuting the concept
of decay.

Wukoki
(Flagstaff, AZ)

A river flowed here
sometimes, and flowers bloomed
along its banks, and animals
came to drink its waters.

The only name it ever had
was the word for "wash."

The boy growing up
in the rock house on the hill
would watch jackrabbits,
deer, coyote, desert rose
rise to life, then slowly die
when the water stayed gone too long.

His father collected water
from the rooftop when the rains came,
saved it in earthen jars.
His mother carried it
five miles from the nearest spring.

Meanwhile he
would crouch on the hill,
against the wall, down in the wash,
among the dry grass,
and no matter the time of day
or year, no matter the presence
or absence of water
he would listen to nothing
but wind urging travel,
saying *to stay here*
is to accept death
as a sooner part of life.

Indian Garden
(Grand Canyon, AZ)

I would live here if I could
where no one expects anything
to live, surrounded by scarcity,
a million years of rock,
and sun among the rock,
and sand among the rock,
and wind among the rock.

When you've traveled this far,
3000 feet, 50 years, and find trees
where there were none before,
and a stream beneath the trees,
and deer beside the stream,
and the absence of guilt or regret,
of anything but exhaustion,
you'll want to stop and lie down
and leave behind
all you thought you knew of leaving.

How To Know the Mountain

You get to know a mountain first
by the shape of the mountain,
each with its own unique profile.
I'd know the mountains around me
no matter where I thought I might be,
Baker's, Grandfather, Table Rock,
Crowders, Hibriten, Pilot.
Sometimes the mountain is named
after its shape, Pickens Nose,
Cesar's Head, Craggy Dome,
Three Top, Hanging Rock, Humpback.
Sometimes after appearance,
Whiteside, Sawtooth, Shining Rock,
Brushy, Flattop, Grassy Ridge Bald.
Sometimes after what the mountain
contains, Hemlock, Chestnut, Sassafras,
Licklog, Chinquapin, Huckleberry Knob.
But there's no knowing a mountain,
until you've actually been on it,
until you've hiked it, climbed it,
breathed its air, listened to what
it has to say, until you've learned
just what the mountain can do to you,
Jumpoff, Gallbuster, Ripshin.

Listening to Louie in the Shadow of Grandfather
(Foscoe, NC)

Like single malt warming the veins,
a fire smoldering low and steady,
a hammock strung between beech trees,
hands around a steaming cup of coffee,
this mountain, familiar and strong
as arms that hold you tight,
voice drawling like that time of dusk
when you know the day is over,
lines hummed in your head on a long road home,
nights we know will become the good old days.

In Praise of Rivers That Flow North
(Fayetteville, WV)

St. Lawrence, Nile, Magdalena.
Some think they do so in defiance
of gravity, convinced the globe
has a certain orientation,
north naturally on top.

Others recognize the flaw
in seeing the world as top heavy
as a Barbie Doll, know celestial
bodies have neither up nor down,
that rivers simply flow

whichever way the land falls.
Traveling up the Rhine,
away from the source,
I fell in love with the Lorelei,
with castles and towers,

with the horseshoe turn at Boppard
and the idea of things that go
by contraries. Lena,
Yenisei, Ob, so many rivers
flow from Southern highlands

to empty themselves
into frozen seas.
There's something to be said for bucking
trends, embracing difference,
denying conventional wisdom.

Chatuge
(Hayesville, NC)

Long fingers of catalpa trees,
green globes of apples
hang low over Licklog Road.

White crowns of Queen Anne's lace,
orange umbels of butterfly weed
fill a field where flycatchers

dart from limb to grass
and back, consuming
whatever rises. Swallows

carve endless angles across
the tops of weeds let go.
Brown headed cowbirds

follow white-faced cows
near a lake surrounded
by mountains in a place

where everyone waves
and everyone remembers
what it means to live.

Treescape
(Cade's Cove, TN)

Sure, there is land.
There is always land,
and sky and probably water
somewhere just out of sight,
but I'm here for the trees,
for the texture they bring,
the depth, the personality,
always different, always
changing, and not just year
to year, but season to season,
even day to day,
and not just outside but inside,
even above and below,
leaves budding, then tender,
curled green of just opening,
then dark green of maturity
and before falling a sequence
of colors unique to each,
and not just the leaves
but limbs and roots endlessly
branching, twisting, turning
to find light, air, water,
creating a design more
unlike anything else
than any snowflake
or fingerprint might be.

"Great," my daughter dismisses,
not sharing my fascination
with trees or my excitement
in dragging her along
on a Sunday country drive,

"Another pretty tree,
and another one, and another one,"
but to me of all I've seen
in 60 years on Earth
nothing impresses as much,
nothing seems as full
of life, of meaning, of beauty,
of connection to all there is
as trees.

Cabin in the Mountains
(Cade's Cove, TN)

It takes a mountain to make us remember
how much of life is color.
Not one, but uncountable trees,
these reds, yellows, greens,
what sustain us, lives
we turn into our lives,
lives we cannot live without.

Shadow Creek
(Cashiers, NC)
after Roethke

Sunday morning, unscripted,
fragrant with coffee,
chatter of water on rock,
I count an impossible number
of trees in one place,
ash and poplar,
hemlock and laurel,
oak and birch,
rhododendron and pine,
maple and Fraser magnolia,
and I remember what I've lost,
what has been forgotten
in the endless hoop of days,
blur of working and cleaning,
striving and getting, taking care,
keeping what has to be kept,
but here, between the sky
seen through trees, the earth
seen through trees, the water
heard and seen through glimpses
between the trees,
some clarity returns,
and I lean again to beginnings,
sheath wet.

Cape Breton
(Nova Scotia)

Bodies of water everywhere,
mountains lopped off at the shore,
steep cliffs and deep river canyons,
windblown, moose-browsed fir and spruce,
islands near and far,
shoals of birds,
morning mist,
white trunks of paper birch.

My eyes are full.
Another one off the list,
and one of the oldest.
My bucket runneth over.

A Decidedly Unscientific Estimation of the Value of Place

I fell in love with words in the second grade at William Blake
Elementary School.

My stepfather drew blood from my legs with a belt buckle
on Davis Avenue.

Another held my hand to the electric stove burner on Edge
field.

Along Highway 24, we chipped off chunks of road and
melted them over an old oil drum to shape our own
roads for Matchbox cars.

I wrote my first poem in the front bedroom at 412 Bond
Street.

I realized I would be okay as a father in a place called
Valmead.

Off Croatan Highway on the Outer Banks I stood one
hundred years later on the exact spot where the
Wright Brothers first left the ground, and as the wind
rose in my face, I cried.

All of these were places made important by what happened
there.

And there have been dozens more.

I remember learning in 10th grade in a high school in
Frankfurt, Germany, about the excavation of the city
of Troy and how they discovered not one city but 9,
one built on top of the other, and thinking clearly that

was an important place situated as it was where two seas, two bodies of land, two cultures came together.

And I know it's fuzzy math, but if I figure in 60 years I've had at least 60 important events that have happened in 60 different places, and given that there have been across history 100 billion people on a planet where the inhabitable surface area is only 25 million square miles, and that most of those 100 billion people have had a similar number of important events, it seems unlikely that there could be a single square foot of Earth where nothing important has ever happened, and more likely that each square foot has been home to an impressive and haunting depth of human experience.

Tanka
(Winston-Salem, NC)

down by muddy creek
pervasive quiet
of bare limbs disturbed
by irrepressible urge
of pear blossoms

Navigation
(Old Fort, NC)

I emerge from the curve near mile marker 75
heading west on I-40, and Black Mountain
looms before me large and dark,
and as I continue the turn the mountains
scroll by, Mitchell and Rattlesnake, Lookout
and Graybeard, Rocky Knob and Pinnacle,
until the entire panorama of the Blue Ridge
is spread out before me, half a billion years
of mountain, older than trees, older
than rivers, older than anything except
the rocks that make them. I roll down my window
and take a deeper breath, and whether it's that
or the Celtic music playing on public radio
from Spindale, something makes me feel
for a moment more alive, more connected,
more certain of the possibility of some place called home.

On a Tree Seen Near Clinton, SC

I've never seen a tree split down the middle
from the top, stump still standing 10 feet
above the ground, limbs broken to every side
but still hanging on like ribs of a stripped umbrella.
What could cause such artistic destruction,
wind, lightning, the weight of pecans pulling
every way at once? In sixty two years
of going out of my way to see things I had never
seen before, I've seen plenty to surprise me.
Still, anytime I've heard the claim, *Now
I've seen it all*, I'm naturally dubious, but now,
I know no matter how long we live, no matter
how much we travel, no matter how much
of the world we see, we can never see it all.

DISCOVERIES MADE LATE IN LIFE

Because Trees Had Always Meant Escape

or fear, he plants them from seed,
mixing coffee grounds with dirt, covering
each with a thin layer of peat,
watering, just a little, each day.

Every part of his mind is a wooded
path. Planting seeds he wanders dark trails
of imagination, letting whatever comes
find him here among the safety of trees.

He keeps them in cups in the window,
covered with cellophane or glass.
He knows the day they go in,
what shape they'll take towards growing.

Even in memory's clenched fist,
green leaves protrude between the fingers.
Everything he opens smells sweet
and corrupt as good earth.

Sometimes he watches for the soil
to shudder, shift, slip to one side
or another, rise on the arching back
of seed pushing to be free.

He is learning the name of every tree
that grows inside him, paper-thin skin
of birch, hermaphrodite magnolia, willow's
swing of weeping, knob-kneed cypress.

With each first appearance above ground,
green cotyledons struggling to slough off
seed, he wants to coach it on growth,

to speak of moisture, seasons, reaching

towards light that warms to this rising.

Joy Comes To Those Who Give It

Twelve birds, two squirrels, wind,
endlessly branching ways
of reaching toward the sky,
embracing what lives below.

What a world to see in trees.
Anyone who has ever lived with one knows
how countless are the things that live in trees,
how endless the ways of giving.

Haiku

Spanish chestnut—
a pricked finger the price
for admiration.

Clearing the Garden

We are all tired and dirty,
our hands thick with digging,
backs wet with bending and rising,
eyes red from sweat
pouring in at the corners.

All day we have pulled up vines,
swung blades across tender necks
of plants, felt the strength
of years pulling back.

We want to make a place
that shines with flowers,
reeks of ripened fruit.

All day we have broken pink flesh
of roots, pulled the threads
that hold things together.

The work blisters up in our palms.
Tools splinter from rough handling.
We have done all we will do today.
It could never be enough.

The sun is still out.
The sky is blue going to red.
I am not ready to go in.
I will stay here a while
and watch the earth shrink
beneath the cool touch
of night's coming on.

Castings

Planting with old
gloves worn thin
in places, bare
in others, hands
become coated
with wet blackness,
dirt and dung,
gray dust of seed
and potash, poisoning
the nose, burning
the eyes, refusing
to be wiped clean.

Grubbing dead earth
and wilted wet leaves,
turning the rotted
smell of mulch and
compost, pink nails turn
black, crack beneath
the force of scratching
dank soil packed
like coffee grounds
between the lines
of living and dead
cells at the end
of worn fingers.

Raising a once-white
hand to sweat-wet lips
I taste the thick diet
of earthworm and mole,
savor the promise
of sweet seeds

the moist pre-birth
beneath the surface.

Interwoven

In the backyard of the new house
in an area 300 feet square
where I want to plant rhododendron,
Japanese maple, Lady Jane magnolia,
I find a network of vines that boggles
the mind, blackberry and vinca, greenbrier
and wisteria, honeysuckle and grape,
and many I cannot name,
planted or let grow by someone
grown tired of gardening, some
traveling 20ft across the ground,
even further beneath the surface in search
of a tree or wall or fence to climb,
anything vertical in their vegetative mind.
Pulling one reveals a dozen more,
layered on top of each other, like some
multi-headed hydra, unending, insidious
as shame, guilt, a sense of unworth,
woven together to form an almost
immovable fabric. I pull vines
with a passion I don't completely understand
for hours at a time, days in a row,
and weeks later still feel
I've gained so little ground,
and only found, an unsought secret
to how unwanted things last.

Late April in North Carolina

Late April in North Carolina surprises me
with a gift of one more day made for flannel.
I put on my black and white plaid and wear it
first to class and then to a poetry reading.

Contrary to poetic belief it has been
far from the cruelest month bringing
not just new beginnings but such diversity
it seems to represent the best of us,

the worst of us, the young and the old,
and everything in between, every season in one
except the coldest of winter, hottest of summer,
calling us out not just to write such lines as these

but to turn the wet ground for planting fennel
and rosemary, lilac and lavender, yarrow and thyme.

Pansies

One has to wonder where they got
their reputation for pansiness.
Purple and proud, or any color
you might imagine, they grow
where they want to grow, despite the cold,
so much unlike their flashy cousins,
impatiens, petunias, scarlet sage,
petals falling off at first frost,
hardly hearty at all.
Keep your prima donna blossoms,
loud and boastful annuals, brief
and barren. I'll take the pansies
of the world, unassuming, resilient,
quietly doing what they know to do.

Haiku

hours after weeding
I still smell
of rosemary

Of Mint and Memory

The smell of mint makes everything feel clean,
clears the senses like bells ringing,
or windchimes, maybe, on a summer day
in 1973, after the war but before
the bomb became too real a thing to ignore.

They say that smell is our most powerful sense,
not the strongest, not the one
we use the most, but the one we find
closest to memory and feeling, the one
most difficult to ignore, resist, overcome.

I've given up patches of my yard to mint
so I'll always have it for tea,
for homemade chocolate chip ice cream,
for the times I need to go back to days
when I didn't know enough to be afraid.

Why Hostas Are Hard to Hate

My neighbor, a good gardener, asked today
if I would like any of his extra hostas.
They have grown so thick, he said, *I need to split them.*
He went on to say, *I offered them to my children,*
but some people just don't like hostas.

I wondered, how anyone could not like hostas?
I've known hostas most of my life
and I struggle to imagine how they might offend.
Too green, too hardy, too luxurious, too diverse?
Less showy than supportive, hostas
complement the plants around them, provide
a backdrop for those that need to stand out.
Hostas are much more seen than heard,
and always pliable to demands and expectations.
They won't keep you up late at night
or wake you too early. They won't pee
on your carpet or leave surprises in the yard.
They tolerate shade better than most,
ask only for a reasonable amount of water.
They don't chew their nails or toss
cigarette butts on the ground. They remain
indifferent to your differences, your religion
or politics, your sexual proclivities or body piercings,
your hair color, even your weird relatives
who visit unannounced. Hostas accept you
for who you are, bad teeth and all.
A hosta has never asked anyone to change.

Thinking of nothing to make me not
want to take his cast off hostas in,
I told him to give me his tired, his poor,
his huddled hostas yearning to breathe free
and I would find a place for them to prosper.

Haiku

early December
sky through empty limbs—
dissection of blue

Why Strawberries Are Best after Walking the Dogs for 3 Miles along the New Urban Trail

Because the flesh gives easily between the teeth, the little seeds providing just enough crunch to know there's something there

Because they are cool and slightly wet from having just been rinsed and provide enough sweet juice to coat the tongue

Because they require no preparation aside from the rinsing

Because in late February and early March in North Carolina what other fruit could be this fresh

Because they make no dishes

Because all that is not consumed, the little green leaves, go willingly into the compost bucket

Because if I avoid the large ones, each one is the perfect size for a single bite

Because they are red and shaped like little hearts

Because they sit quietly on the counter just waiting

Because eating strawberries always seems indulgent and sometimes a little sensual

Because they are neither fruit nor berry but part of the flower itself

Because when my lungs are expanding with life, my eyes still full of all I've just seen, little else could make me feel more alive

Discoveries Made Late in Life

I went out today to discover something,
anything, knowing the world
still has plenty to show me.
I noticed how certain lilies
can spring 2 ft out of the ground
and flower without a leaf or branch.
And then, a student, who named herself
after an insect, and considers herself
neither male nor female and attracted to both
joined me and pointed out
in a nameless garden next
to a building that was given a name
how bugleweed has the same dark beauty
as certain ornamental grasses.

I begin to imagine a world
where time's not wasted
on feeling ashamed of being
black, gay, trans, male, female, uncertain,
where time's not wasted
on hiding the facts of how
you feel about who you are,
where time's not wasted
on fearing that someone else
might be different than you.
I begin to imagine a world
where there's so much more time
for thinking, loving, making, sharing.

I went out today to discover something.
I had not thought to find anything in particular
but noticed despite my years of living and looking,

that so many things remain unexpected
and probably will remain so until I look for them.

Rehousing

We planted a weeping cherry,
maybe 6 ft tall,
in the front yard of the house
my father-in-law bought 15 years ago.
We placed a wooden bird box
where limbs were grafted to trunk.
That first spring, a bluebird
made her nest there.
And for three years, she,
or another like her, did so
again, until bulging branches
turned the box sideways
and locked it into place
as if the box had grown
as just a part of the tree
burl, knot, strange fruit.

The box was largely forgotten
and went unoccupied for years
as the tree continued to grow
above it and around it, leaving
at last only the opening visible,
the rest covered in limbs and bark.
But this fall, my father-in-law
gone to assisted living,
his home bought by us,
I see again, as I've seen before,
how nature reclaims all
it once owned or made use of,
as chickadees, tufts of straw
between their beaks, begin to move in.

Gardening at 60

Crouch a little,
until your ankles hurt;
bend a little,
until your back hurts;
kneel a little,
until your knees hurt;

stand up; stretch;
crouch again;
bend again;
kneel again.
Dig your fingers
into soil.
Raise your arms
to sky.
Pray for rain.

Be realistic.
Don't try to do it
all in one day.
Be realistic.
Nobody needs
20 tomato plants,
10 hills of cucumbers,
any number of cauliflower.

Knee pads are your friend,
and anything with a long handle.
Hum a little, or sing.
Whistle at least.
Settle in.
Let it be meditative,
therapeutic.

Think of how good
what you've grown
with your own hands
will taste, how you'll know
exactly what went into it
or didn't. No DDT,
BPA, GMO,
whatever other initials
might be discovered
before this poem is published.

Mostly, enjoy
not just the fruits
of your labor,
but the labor itself.

Tanka

grandchild in stroller
60 minute walk
along wooded trail
neither makes an unhappy
peep

Difference of Opinion

The Sunday morning walker,
seeing me on my knees again,
says, *Good morning*, and then,
meaning to empathize with hard
work, arthritic hands,
aching backs and knees,
remarks, *It never ends, does it?*
meaning the pulling of weeds,
gathering of leaves, replacement
of violets with creeping thyme.
I understand her good intentions,
but see it differently, and so reply,
No, I guess it never does.
Thank goodness for that.

All That Is

It's winter,
a hard time of year
for noticing things,
except the wide sky
through limbs of trees,
and the shapes of trees
stripped of leaves,
and a white-breasted nuthatch
hopping sideways
down the trunk
of a peeling paper birch,
and the omnipresent cold,
and the quiet
of everyone staying inside
as long as they possibly can,
but all that is not there,
in the haunted austerity
of a winter landscape,
is what makes it possible
to see all that is

The Winter Day
after Mary Oliver

I stand up from my work,
which is never ending,
and which I would have no other way,
to look out the window.
It is February in North Carolina.
Snow has fallen.
Barely half an inch,
but enough to cover the ground
and lie on top of evergreen
limbs, cupped in leaves
of holly and euonymous,
coating horizontal branches
of cherry trees and cedar.
The sun is out now
and illuminates everything,
and so are the birds,
finches and juncos,
white-throated sparrow,
flitting from place to place,
excited at the opportunities
afforded them to forage
on seeds and berries.
The contrast of green
and white is remarkable
and hypnotic. I stand
and look much longer
than intended, until I remember
this opportunity afforded me
is why I sit at my desk
to begin with.

Sound Effect

Head down, planting bulbs,
the sound of leaves rustling by on asphalt
so much like bicycle tires on Bond Street
fifty years ago that I have to look up
to make sure it's not Tracy Harbison
on his way to baseball in Matthews Mill Village Cemetery,
or Chuck Davis speeding away
from someone he insulted, someone twice
his size, proving himself as he felt
he had to prove himself every day,
or God forbid Beth Thomas
whose long lashes batted my way
could always change my mind about
just about anything including the likelihood
of these dreams of the past recurring
now if not here then at least
in some place I might be soon to go.

Haiku

quiet day, barely
a tremble among the leaves,
just patterns of light

ANY NEW THING THAT MATTERS

At Ivey Memorial Cemetery, Maiden, NC

How many names should a cemetery have?
From here I count 2 Longs, 2 Gladdens,
2 Fowlers, 2 Dills, 2 Loftins, 6 Drums,
6 Ballards, and 15 Goodsons, a solitary Poe,
Whiteside, Lawing, Henry, and Keever.
Is that too many? Too few? Too unbalanced?
A little more than a family plot.
But I've seen smaller, and much larger too.

Is there a right number? Is there
such a thing as cemetery etiquette?
If so, I'm sure we broke the rules as kids
playing baseball in the cemetery
in Mathews Mill Village, one headstone
the backstop, a footstone for each base,
and at night, there was the irreverence of Ghost
in the Graveyard in the actual graveyard.

I remember the cemetery at the Chapel of Rest
in Patterson, North Carolina. Most
of the headstones worn blank, names
and dates, last words and epitaphs
silenced, lost to rain and weather.
Even the angels had lost their faces.

And I've trembled at rows upon rows
of identical headstones or crosses,
in unimaginable numbers in straight lines
from every angle at Arlington and Normandy.

I drive through Oakwood Cemetery,
where I taught my boys to drive,
each day after teaching to avoid

the slow down at Oakwood Elementary School.
I hope to avoid cemeteries when I die,
not dying, of course. I understand
the inevitability of that. Just
the prolonged permanence of death
in a sealed box, under ground, in a place like a cemetery.

I intend to die

on my feet
looking at something beautiful
or interesting or new,
but not anytime in the near
future, mind you.
In fact, if I could live
forever, I would,
but only if I could maintain
enough vitality to hike
at least the easy trails,
enough cognition to appreciate
what I could see,
birds and trees,
the freshness of youth,
a new idea,
a new connection,
any new thing that matters.

I intend to die
on my feet
unless of course
I happen to be
on my knees
planting another tree
when my time comes
to cease to be.

Kouta

early morning sky
puts itself together again
with every patch of light
the clouds can't hold back

About the Author

Scott Owens is the author of 24 collections of poetry and a recipient of awards from the Academy of American Poets, the Pushcart Prize Anthology, the Next Generation/Indie Lit Awards, the North Carolina Writers Network, the North Carolina Poetry Society, and the Poetry Society of South Carolina. His poems have been featured on *The Writer's Almanac* eight times, and his articles about writing poetry have been used in *Poet's Market* four times. He has been twice nominated for the National Book Critics Circle Award and for North Carolina Poet Laureate. Owens holds degrees from Ohio University, the University of North Carolina at Charlotte, and the University of North Carolina at Greensboro. He is Professor of Poetry at Lenoir-Rhyne University and a former editor of *Wild Goose Poetry Review* and *Southern Poetry Review*. He owns and operates Taste Full Beans Coffeehouse and Gallery and coordinates Poetry Hickory in Hickory, NC.

www.ingramcontent.com/pod-product-compliance
Lightning Source LLC
Chambersburg PA
CBHW031139090426
42738CB00008B/1153